T0245916

THE BARTENDER'S GUIDE TO

RUM

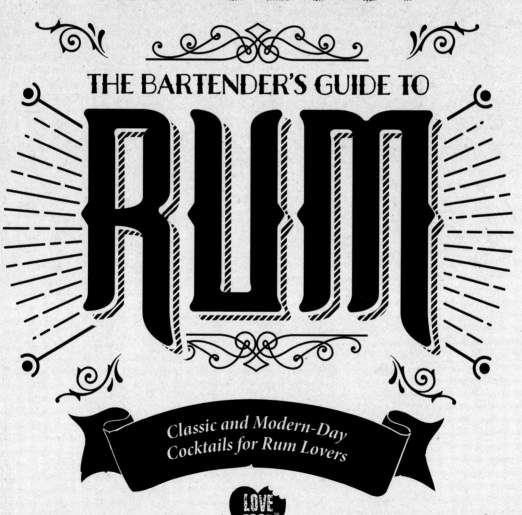

THE ART OF

· MIXOLOGY ·

THE BARTENDER'S GUIDE TO

RUM

Classic and Modern-Day
Cocktails for Rum Lovers

LOVE
FOOD™

CONTENTS

A BRIEF HISTORY of RUM

The evolution of rum has been shaped by various historical events spanning many centuries, from purely medicinal use, to the dark years of slavery and pirates, to the rum cocktails we know today crafted by modern mixologists. One element remains at the heart of the story—but what other factors came into play in rum's spirited history?

Rum, like all distilled spirits, shares a common ancestor in the first stills that were filled by Arabic alchemists as early as the first century. This was when the Roman Empire was in full swing and Christianity appeared. These early scientists spent decades distilling all manner of elixirs, gleaning knowledge from the Greeks, amongst other sources.

By the twelfth century, the knowledge had spread further across Europe and was being nurtured in the hands of Benedictine monks in Salerno, Italy. At this point, spirit was utilized purely for medicinal and scientific reasons, being used to preserve rare and precious ingredients used in medicine. From Italy, the science of distillation began to grow through the monasteries, right across Europe and the known world. The process was still crude, but over the centuries it was continuously improved by Europe's scientific minds. By the seventeenth century, distillation was in full swing and we began to see the commercialization of distilled spirits.

Of all the commodities of the ancient and modern world, sugar is undoubtedly amongst the most significant, shaping empires and the very trade routes and shipping lanes that are still used today. The importance of sugar cultivation in the ancient world right through into the twenty-first century cannot be understated. Where sugar has been cultivated, rum production has nearly always followed.

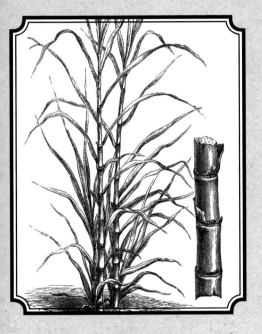

The precise origins of the very first distilled spirits derived from sugarcane are uncertain, but the birth of rum as we know it can find its roots in the sugarcane plantations of the Caribbean, cultivated by the Portuguese, Dutch, French, and English empires as early as the sixteenth century.

Throughout the sixteenth century, Europe was developing an incredibly sweet tooth and a fondness for sweetness that is still very much alive today. The climate and soils in the Caribbean suited sugarcane perfectly and, with very small indigenous populations, the

islands and their population were subjected to exploitation by these larger empires. For the next two centuries, the colonial plantations of the Caribbean, as well as plantations in South America, would provide 90 percent of the growing demand for sugar in Europe.

It was Christopher Columbus who first introduced sugarcane to the Caribbean on his second voyage to the Americas in 1493. One of the consequences of the creation of links between Europe, the Caribbean, and the Americas was the African slave trade.

The trade triangle between Europe, the Caribbean, and the Americas was formed, where sugar, molasses, and rum were shipped from the Caribbean into Europe and the Americas. Rum and European goods were then shipped to Africa and traded for African people, who were in turn sold as slaves and sent to the Caribbean and the Americas to work on plantations. It's estimated that more than 11 million Africans were forced into slavery and were taken on ships heading to the Americas to work on plantations between the sixteenth and nineteenth centuries.

With so much rum being shipped around the world at this time, rum and molasses started to be used as currency and became synonymous with the Royal Navy and as a drink of privateers. During the 1700s, the power and influence of the sugar trade was growing, reaching into the UK parliament with powerful lobbyists championing rum as a noble and exotic alternative to spirits such as gin and brandy, both of which were suffering major reputational damage due to associations with war and poverty.

It was rum's time to shine and with a solid supply of molasses and spirits from the colonies, rums that were produced in the Caribbean, New England, and Bristol and London began to flow into the glasses of the British aristocracy and middle classes, normally in the form of a spiced punch.

With the abolition of slavery during the 1800s, the production of Caribbean sugar fell and so did the molasses that was being used to make rum. The French responded by producing large volumes of sugar domestically from beets and, for the first time, rum began to rival sugar in value as an article of trade. Throughout the 1800s, major advances in distillation and a better understanding of barrel-aging emerged, and the quality of rum as a whole improved dramatically.

In the first half of the twentieth century, the Scottish and Irish whiskey industries were slowing down. They were starved of the grains they needed to produce whiskey due to the two World Wars. With molasses being a by-product of the sugar industry and having no use as a foodstuff, the production of rum continued.

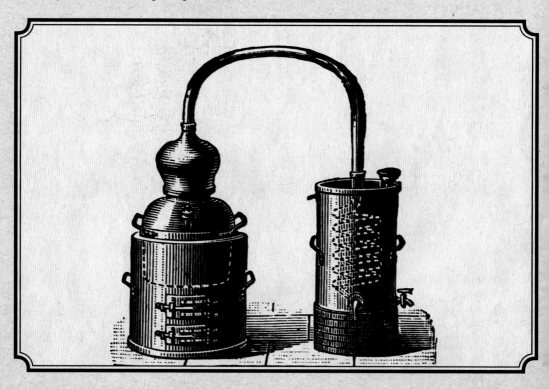

In more recent years, rums of very high quality are being produced by distillers all over the world, but Caribbean rum in particular has started to gain international recognition by spirit experts.

Nearly 400 years since the first rums were produced in the Caribbean, rum is finally taking its rightful place as one of the world's finest spirits alongside prestigious whiskies and cognacs. A mighty journey and eventful history can be found in every glass of rum, no matter where it's from.

Rum producers seized the opportunity to fill the empty glasses, quenching the thirst for strong spirits. With the rise of Tiki bars and cocktails, the popularity of rum was growing and moving away from its dark past and associations with slavery.

In the 1960s the West Indies Rum & Spirits Producers' Association (WIRSPA) was set up to help promote and protect the interests of its member distilleries and help in the marketing and export of Caribbean rum worldwide. More recently WIRSPA set up the Authentic Caribbean Rum marque (ACR) with the goal to create a visual symbol to help the identification of genuine Caribbean rums.

PRODUCTION *of* RUM

All complex, flavorful spirits can boast a varied and diverse production process, but none more so than rum. Being made all over the world, the production of rum (or sugarcane-based spirits) and the techniques used in distillation are almost infinite. To best understand rum, you first need to have an understanding of how alcohol is made.

All alcoholic drinks are the product of a serendipitous relationship between yeast and sugar. Yeast is a single-cell organism and a fungus which, within the right conditions, can transform the fermentable sugars in a sugary liquid into alcohol. The origin of the base liquid will determine the type of beverage being made. In the case of rum, the base liquid is either made from molasses or pure sugarcane juice. The art of fermentation has been manipulated by man for thousands of years and evolved

into the different alcoholic beverages we see today. This is a fortuitous relationship that has been at the heart of many civilizations and cultures, both ancient and modern.

In its simplest form rum is produced by fermenting molasses or pure sugarcane juice to make an alcoholic solution known as wash. This can then be taken forward to distillation in either pot or column stills, or both. Following distillation some producers will then mature their rums in oak casks, further mellowing the spirit with complex flavors found in oak. Most rums start life as molasses which is a by-product of sugarcane. Sugarcane is harvested and pressed to release the cane juice. The juice is then boiled on a series of pots reducing the solution to a syrup. After the final boiling stage, the remaining syrupy liquid is left to cool. At this point sugar crystals will begin to form, leaving behind a thick, dark liquid known as molasses.

Next, the molasses is then usually diluted with water and then fermented to create an alcoholic solution known as wash. This step in production can vary enormously between producers. Different yeast strains and fermentation times can have a big impact in forming different flavors. After fermentation a wash of around 8% ABV will be taken forward to be distilled. The types of still used varies from distillery to distillery. With each still capable of creating a unique distillate, the door is kicked open to almost limitless variations.

Pot stills help create a richer and more flavorful liquor, whereas column stills will strip out more impurities in the spirit creating a lighter style. In some cases, stills involving both pots and columns are used.

During distillation, the distiller will isolate the sweet spot in the spirit run, known as the middle cut or heart of the run. This will then be taken forward to maturation or bottling. In the case of white rums, it's usually straight to the bottling plant with the liquor. But if maturation is on the cards, then the process is much more interesting.

Oak casks that have previously held bourbon or sherry are typically used. However, where maturation can vary greatly is in the climate where the casks will rest. The immense heat in the Caribbean can create a rapid maturation effect as the liquor expands and is forced into the pores of the oak. As it cools and the liquor retracts, it brings with it lactones and flavor compounds from the cask, which bring both a deep and interesting flavor and color.

The downside to the intense heat is the evaporation of the liquor from the casks, known as, "the angels' share". In some rum distilleries as much as 10 percent a year can be lost to evaporation. To try to slow it down, some producers will mature their rums in cooler warehouses. In some extreme cases, they might even move casks up mountains or underground.

In a perfect world, all aged rums would be natural color, but this is rarely the case. Prior to bottling, many rum producers sweeten their rum in a way similar to that used by cognac producers. Regulations on how much sugar can be added back into the rum prior to bottling vary, but in many cases permitted amounts sit at about 5 percent. This might not sound like a lot, but it can have a big impact on the final liquor in the bottle—and not always in a good way.

Ahead of bottling, vatting has to be considered. If the producer has several still types and a large inventory of aged stocks, casks of various ages and spirit types will be combined. This is done to create a uniform style and help achieve consistency from batch to batch.

Where rum excels in production is in the use of combined and hybrid stills. Their production process can be fantastically complex, requiring master distillers with immense skill and attention to detail.

TYPES *of* RUM

With an almost infinite number of production twists and cultural turns, the idea of what rum is and how it's made can vary greatly. Unlike most other liquors, rum remains undefined by a complete set of industry definitions. Production methods considered normal practice in one country or distillery may be considered sacrilege in another. But where some may see rum as an undefinable giant of the liquor industry, others see an untamable charm.

GLOBAL CATEGORIES

White Rums

Nearly always unaged and often deemed inferior to dark/aged rums, white rums are the usual choice for most backbars and often seen as vodka's slightly better-looking sister. However, some fantastic white rums can be found, and in some cases producers will actually take aged spirit through a charcoal filtration process to remove the color, producing white rums with greater depth of flavor.

Dark Rums

Drawing their color from barrel-aging and usually based on molasses as opposed to pure sugarcane juice, the dark rum category is vast. It encompasses rums of high quality to the bottom-shelf varieties. Sometimes the cheaper varieties will be unaged liquor darkened with caramel and sweetened prior to bottling. This might be done to give the illusion of aging in casks.

Navy Rums

A blend of dark rums, typically built around rums from Guyana and usually originating from distilleries found in the British West Indies. Navy Rum became synonymous with dark rum and vice versa during its rise in popularity with the Royal Navy in the nineteenth century. Navy-strength rums would fall into the overproof bracket below.

Overproof Rums

In the United States, the minimum proof is 40% ABV, whereas in the European Union (EU), the minimum strength for bottling rum is 37.5% ABV. The term "overproof" refers to rums with a higher-than-usual bottling strength and typically 50–70% ABV. Before the use of hydrometers, alcohol strength in liquors was simply measured by using gunpowder in what was known as "the gunpowder test." A small amount of gunpowder would be soaked in the liquor, then a spark of flame would be put to the powder. If it ignited, the liquor would be proven, and therefore considered overproof. In short, "overproof," in modern terms, means wickedly strong.

Spiced Rums

The quality and quantity of additives used to sweeten and flavor spiced rums vary greatly between the different varieties. Mainstream and cheaper spiced rums are usually flavored and colored heavily using sugar, spices, and caramel. In extreme cases some are so heavily laced with flavoring, that they can't technically qualify as rum in some markets. Despite leaning more toward a liqueur than a true rum, the "spiced" style has become popular when served with mixers, such as cola or ginger beer.

RUM, BUT NOT RUM

Rhum Agricole

Originating from the island of Martinique and the French West Indies, this style of rum takes its cues from the French colonials and can only be made from domestic cane crops and the resulting pure cane juice. Rhum Agricole is the only cane-derived liquor to carry an Appellation d'Origine Contrôlée mark (AOC), a mark usually reserved for French wine producers. Some of the finest distillates on the planet can be found in this category.

Cachaça

Cachaça is Brazil's answer to rum, and taking its name from the Dutch word for sugarcane. Cachaça is made from only pure cane juice and is, in principal, similar to the Agricole style of the French West Indies. However, production differences surrounding alcohol strength, origins of their cane, and distillation strengths mean they are, in fact, quite different. Some of the planets biggest distilleries are making cachaça, but finding truly great examples of this liquor outside of Brazil can be difficult.

Indian Rum and Asia

Various countries are producing vast amounts of sugar and therefore, molasses. This is fermented and made into spirit, again of various styles using pot and column stills in distilleries big and small. In many cases, these distillates are destined to be sold domestically, and—to make things more confusing—are sometimes blended with small amounts of grain-based spirit and labeled as whiskey. Some producers do label their blends as rum, however, and they are fantastic to drink.

GLASSWARE

It is important to serve a cocktail in the appropriate glass—the size, shape, and style all have an impact on the visual perception and enjoyment of the drink. Here are some of the classic glasses that you will need to have in your collection.

Martini Glass

The most iconic of all cocktail glasses, the conical martini glass emerged with the art deco movement. The long stem is perfect for chilled drinks, it keeps people's hands from inadvertently warming the cocktail.

Highball Glass

Sometimes also known as a Collins glass, these glasses are perfect for serving drinks with a high proportion of mixer to alcohol.

Old-Fashioned Glass

The old-fashioned glass, also known as a rocks glass, is a short, squat tumbler and is great for serving any liquor on the rocks, or for short, mixed cocktails.

Champagne Flute

The tall, thin flute's tapered design reduces the champagne's surface area and so helps to keep the fizz in the drink for longer.

Shot Glass

This glass is a home bar essential and can hold just enough alcohol to be drunk in one mouthful. The shot glass can also stand in for 1½ ounces when making cocktails.

Margarita Glass

This wide-rimmed glass, as its name indicates, is used to serve margaritas and daiquiris.

Coupe Glass

Another wide-rimmed glass that is good for serving sparkling drinks. The short-stemmed coupe is also used for serving daiquiris.

Snifter Glass

The bowl-shaped snifter glass invites the drinker to cradle the drink in their hands, warming the contents of the glass. The aroma of the drink is held in the glass, letting you breathe it in before sipping the drink.

Hurricane Glass

This pear-shaped glass pays homage to the hurricane lamp and was the glass used to create the New Orleans rum-based hurricane cocktail. It's also used for a variety of frozen and blended cocktails.

Iced Beverage Glass

A variation on the highball glass, this is a design classic that is used to serve Long Island iced tea and the mojito. Its tall body and short stem make it ideal for chilled drinks.

What equipment you have in your home bar depends on whether you like all the latest gadgets, or whether you are prepared to make do with some basic options. Nowadays, there is no limit to the amount of bar equipment available, but you don't need

a lot of gimmicky gadgets to make most of the beverages in this book. Here are some of the essential tools of the trade that you'll need.

Jiggers

A jigger is a bartender's basic measuring tool and essential for crafting the perfect blend of ingredients. It usually has a measurement on each end, such as 1 ounce and 1½ ounces. Get a steel jigger with clear measurement markings so you can easily and accurately pour out measurements.

Barspoon

A barspoon has a small bowl and a long handle that allows you to muddle, mix, and stir with ease. Spoons come in a variety of lengths and widths. A stylishly designed barspoon is an attractive addition to any bartender's kit.

Shaker

Most contemporary shakers are made from stainless steel because it doesn't tarnish or conduct heat easily. It is useful for chilled cocktails because the ice cools the cocktail rather than the shaker. Most standard shakers come with a built-in strainer, but if you're using a Boston or Parisian shaker, you'll need to use a separate strainer.

Mixing Glass

Any vessel that holds about 2 cups of liquid can be used for mixing drinks. It is good to have a mixing glass with a spout so you can stop ice from slipping into the glass.

Mixing glasses are increasingly popular and are usually made of glass or crystal.

Muddler

For mashing up citrus fruit or crushing herbs, you need a muddler. This is a chunky wooden tool with a rounded end; it can also be used to make cracked ice.

Strainer

A bar or Hawthorne strainer is an essential tool to prevent ice and other ingredients being poured into your glass. Some cocktails need to be double strained, so even if there is a strainer in your cocktail shaker, you'll still need a separate Hawthorne strainer.

Juicer

A traditional juicer, with a ridged half-lemon shape on a saucer, works perfectly well for juicing small amounts. There is also a citrus spout that screws into a lemon or lime and is useful for obtaining tiny amounts of juice.

Other Equipment

Other items you might need are: corkscrew, bottle opener, cocktail sticks, blender, tongs, ice bucket, chopping board, knives, pitchers, swizzle sticks, and straws.

TECHNIQUES

Shaking and Stirring

These are the two most basic mixology techniques, but they are essential to master in order to make any cocktail with confidence.

Shaking is when you add all the ingredients, with the specified amount of ice cubes, to the shaker and then shake vigorously for 5–10 seconds. The benefits of shaking are that the drink is rapidly mixed, chilled, and aerated. Once the drink has been shaken, the outside of the shaker should be lightly frosted.

Shaking a cocktail also dilutes the drink significantly. This dilution is essential because it gives the correct balance of taste, strength, and temperature. The drink is then double strained into glasses—the shaker should have a built-in strainer and you usually use a separate strainer over the glass as well. Shaking can also be used to prepare cocktails that include an ingredient, such as an egg white, that will not combine with less vigorous forms of mixing.

Stirring is the purist's choice—it's where you add all the ingredients, usually with some ice cubes, but this time you combine them in a mixing glass or beaker and then stir the ingredients together using a barspoon or swizzle stick. As with shaking, this allows you to blend and chill the ingredients without too much erosion of the ice, so you can control the level of dilution and keep it to a minimum.

Building and Layering

Building is a mixology technique, a technical term for the task of pouring all the ingredients, one by one, usually over ice, into the glass in which the cocktail will be served. You might then stir the cocktail briefly, but this is just to mix rather than for chilling or aerating. It is important to follow recipes exactly, as the order of the ingredients can change from drink to drink and this can affect the final flavor.

Another important skill that a bartender must acquire is the art of layering, which requires greater precision and a steadier hand. To make layered shooters or other drinks, you generally pour the heaviest liquid first, working through to the lightest. However, the real trick is the technique. Either touch the top of the drink with a long-handled barspoon and pour the liquid slowly over the back of it to disperse it across the top of the ingredients already in the glass, or pour the liquid down the twisted stem that many barspoons have. You should hold the spoon's flat disc just above the drink. Be sure to use a clean barspoon for each layer. Floating is the term used to describe adding the top layer.

Muddling and Blending

Muddling is the term used to describe the extraction of the juice or oils from the pulp or skin of a fruit, herb, or spice. It involves mashing ingredients to release their flavors and it's usually done with a muddler.

As the name suggests, blending is when all the ingredients are combined in a blender. This technique is often used when mixing alcohol with fruit or with creamy ingredients that do not combine well unless they are blended. These drinks are often blended with crushed or cracked ice to produce cocktails with a smooth, frozen consistency. Popular blended drinks are frozen daiquiris and coladas.

Chapter 1

CLASSIC CONCOCTIONS

The classics can be relied on time and time again. Steeped in history, tried and tested by rum lovers across the world, these are the staple players on the cocktail menu. Here you'll find favorites, like the Banana Rum Cooler, Mojito, Piña Colada, and Hurricane. They combine traditional flavors and techniques, perfected by bartenders over the years, and many form the basis of some of the new twists we see in modern cocktail bars today.

MOJITO

Serves 1

Ingredients

1 teaspoon simple syrup

few mint leaves, plus extra to garnish

juice of ½ lime, plus lime slice to garnish

1¾ ounces Jamaican rum

club soda

1 dash Angostura bitters

1. Put the syrup, mint leaves, and lime juice in a chilled cocktail glass and crush or muddle the mint leaves.

2. Add ice and the rum, then top off with club soda to taste.

3. Finish with a dash of Angostura bitters and garnish with the mint leaves and lime slice.

PIÑA COLADA

Serves 1

Ingredients

1¾ ounces white rum

¾ ounce dark rum

2½ ounces pineapple juice

1¾ ounces coconut cream

pineapple wedges, to garnish

1. Put the crushed ice in a blender with the white rum, dark rum, pineapple juice, and coconut cream and blend until smooth.

2. Strain, without stirring, into a chilled cocktail glass and garnish with pineapple wedges.

DAIQUIRI

Serves 1

—

Ingredients

1¾ ounces white rum

¾ ounce lime juice

½ teaspoon simple syrup

lime wedge, to garnish

1. Shake the rum, lime juice, and simple syrup over cracked ice until well frosted.

2. Strain into a chilled cocktail glass filled with ice. Garnish with a lime wedge.

DARK & STORMY

Serves 1

—

Ingredients

1¾ ounces golden rum

¾ ounce lime juice

½ ounce simple syrup

ginger beer

lime slice, to garnish

1. Shake the golden rum, lime juice, and simple syrup over cracked ice until well frosted. Strain into a chilled cocktail glass filled with ice and top off with ginger beer to taste.

2. Garnish with a lime slice.

HURRICANE

Serves 1

—

Ingredients

2 ounces dark rum

2 ounces light rum

¾ ounce lemon juice

1¾ ounces orange juice

1¾ ounces passion fruit juice

½ ounce simple syrup

1 teaspoon grenadine

orange slices and cocktail
cherries, to garnish

1. Shake all the liquid ingredients over cracked ice until well frosted.

2. Strain into a chilled cocktail glass filled with ice.

3. Garnish with the orange slices and cherries.

EL PRESIDENTE

Serves 1

Ingredients

1¾ ounces white rum

¾ ounce dry vermouth

¾ ounce dry curaçao

1 dash grenadine

1 cocktail cherry and orange peel, to garnish

1. Shake the white rum, vermouth, and curaçao with a dash of grenadine over cracked ice until well frosted.

2. Strain into a chilled cocktail glass, add a cherry to the base, and garnish the top of the glass with orange peel.

HISTORY *of the* MOJITO

The most famous rum cocktail that's available in almost every cocktail bar, the mojito is a simple combination of white rum, mint, lime, and soda that makes a refreshing hit in warmer climates.

The classic mojito can trace its origins all the way back to the early sixteenth century, when a drink began to emerge in Cuba called the Draque. This was a drink carved into history by none other than Sir Francis Drake, the famous privateer charged by Queen Elizabeth I of England to raid Spanish ships and cities in the emerging colonies.

It was upon Drake's arrival to Cuba in the 1580s that the drink is first referenced. Drake's ship was anchored offshore Havana, and the city's inhabitants watched and waited for what they thought was an inevitable attack. However, Drake's crew were suffering from numerous illnesses and it's believed that a small party of the men went ashore to Havana and collected the classic mojito ingredients as medicine. To the relief of the city and its officials, the attack never came and Drake sailed away. How the drink took its name from the event is uncertain, but what is known is that a beverage using sugarcane spirit, water, mint, and sugar was being consumed for medicinal reasons.

BANANA RUM COOLER

Serves 1

—

Ingredients

1¼ ounces white rum

1¼ ounces pineapple juice

1 banana, peeled and sliced

juice of 1 lime

lime peel twist, to garnish

1. Put cracked ice, the white rum, pineapple juice
and banana into a blender. Add the lime juice
and blend until smooth.

2. Strain into a chilled cocktail glass filled with ice.

3. Garnish with lime peel.

CLASSIC RUM PUNCH

Serves 1

—

Ingredients

¾ ounce fresh lime juice

1¼ ounces simple syrup

1¾ ounces golden rum

lime curls, to garnish

1. Shake the lime juice, simple syrup,
and golden rum over cracked ice until well frosted.

2. Strain into a chilled cocktail glass filled with ice.
Garnish with a long lime curl.

THE RUM RANCH

Serves 1

Ingredients

1 slice seeded red chili, plus extra piece to garnish

1¾ ounces golden rum

2 teaspoons simple syrup

2 teaspoons fresh lemon juice

2 teaspoons fresh orange juice

1 dash Angostura bitters or Pimento bitters

orange and lemon slices, to garnish

1. Add the red chili to the base of a cocktail shaker and muddle, or use the end of a rolling pin, to release the flavor.

2. Add the golden rum, simple syrup, and fruit juices to the shaker with a few drops of Angostura bitters and a handful of cracked ice. Shake vigorously until well frosted, then strain into a chilled cocktail glass filled with ice.

3. Garnish with orange and lemon slices and a piece of red chili.

MAE NAM

Serves 1

Ingredients

1 ¾ ounces golden rum

2 tablespoons fresh lime juice

1 tablespoon Aromatic
Simple Syrup (see below)

1 lemongrass stalk, trimmed and
halved lengthwise, to garnish

AROMATIC SIMPLE SYRUP

½ cup firmly packed
light brown sugar

½ cup water

4-inch piece lemongrass,
halved lengthwise

½-inch piece fresh ginger,
peeled and sliced

red chili

1. To make the aromatic simple syrup, add the sugar and water to a small saucepan, then add the lemongrass, ginger, and chili. Heat gently, stirring occasionally until the sugar has dissolved, then boil for 1 minute. Leave to cool for at least 1 hour for the flavors to infuse, then strain the mixture through a piece of cheesecloth. Pour into a sterilized, sealable jar.

2. To make the cocktail, shake the golden rum, lime juice, and ½ ounce of the Aromatic Simple Syrup over cracked ice until well frosted. The rest of the syrup can be stored in the refrigerator for up to a week.

3. Strain into a chilled cocktail glass filled with ice. Garnish with the lemongrass.

LONG ISLAND ICED TEA

Serves 1

Ingredients

¾ ounce vodka

¾ ounce gin

¾ ounce white tequila

¾ ounce white rum

½ ounce white crème de menthe

1¾ ounces lemon juice

1 teaspoon superfine sugar

cola

lime wedge, to garnish

1. Shake the vodka, gin, tequila, white rum, white crème de menthe, and lemon juice over cracked ice until well frosted. Add the sugar and shake vigorously.

2. Strain into a chilled cocktail glass filled with ice.

3. Top off with cola and garnish with a lime wedge.

JAMAICAN MULE

Serves 1

—

Ingredients

1¾ ounces Jamaican rum

ginger beer

squeeze of lime juice

lime slice, to garnish

1. Pour the Jamaican rum into a chilled
cocktail glass filled with ice.

2. Top off with ginger beer, add a squeeze of lime,
and garnish with a lime slice.

MELLOW MULE

Serves 1

—

Ingredients

1¾ ounces white rum

¾ ounce dark rum

¾ ounce golden rum

¾ ounce falernum

¾ ounce lime juice

ginger beer

fruit slices, to garnish

1. Shake the white rum, dark rum, golden rum, falernum, and lime juice over cracked ice until well frosted.

2. Strain into chilled cocktail glasses.

3. Top off with ginger beer and garnish with fruit slices.

HOT BUTTERED RUM

Serves 1

—

Ingredients

¾ ounce dark rum

1 teaspoon packed
dark brown sugar

5 ounces hot water

1 teaspoon salted butter

¼ teaspoon allspice

1. In an old-fashioned glass, mix together the rum,
brown sugar, and hot water with a teaspoon
until the sugar has completely dissolved.

2. Place the butter on top. Sprinkle with the allspice.

3. Serve when the butter has melted.

MAI TAI

Serves 1

—

Ingredients

¾ ounce white rum

¾ ounce dark rum

¾ ounce orange curaçao

¾ ounce lime juice

1 tablespoon orgeat

1 tablespoon grenadine

fruit slices, to garnish

1. Shake the white and dark rums, curaçao,
lime juice, orgeat, and grenadine vigorously
over cracked ice until well frosted.

2. Strain into a chilled cocktail glass and garnish with fruit slices.

Chapter 2

SIMPLE NOTES

Sometimes simplicity is best. Stylish combinations of lavish, expertly blended ingredients have rightly earned their place on the modern cocktail menu, but pared-back drinks that offer clean flavors are a lighter alternative. Just take a handful of ingredients, some good-quality rum, and blend for understated perfection. Try the famous Cuba Libre, as well as gems like Rum 'n' Currant, Lounge Lizard, and Fox Trot.

PEACH DREAMER

Serves 1

Ingredients

¾ ounce white rum

¾ ounce peach schnapps

2½ ounces fresh orange juice

¾ ounce grenadine

1. Shake the white rum, peach schnapps, and orange juice well over ice. Strain into a chilled cocktail glass filled with ice.

2. Slowly pour a little grenadine into the glass.

OLD SOAK

Serves 1

Ingredients

1¾ ounces golden rum

¾ ounce whiskey liqueur

¾ ounce ginger syrup

club soda

1. Shake the golden rum, whiskey liqueur, and ginger syrup over cracked ice until well frosted.

2. Pour into a chilled cocktail glass filled with ice. Top off with club soda to taste.

CUBA LIBRE

Serves 1

Ingredients

1¾ ounces white rum

cola

lime wedge, to garnish

1. Half-fill a chilled cocktail glass with cracked ice.

2. Pour over the rum and top off with cola.

3. Stir gently to mix and garnish with a lime wedge.

FOX TROT

Serves 1

Ingredients

juice of ½ lemon or 1 lime

2 dashes orange curaçao

1¾ ounces white rum

orange slice, to garnish

1. Shake the lemon juice, orange curaçao, and white rum over cracked ice until well frosted.

2. Strain into a chilled cocktail glass filled with ice. Garnish with an orange slice.

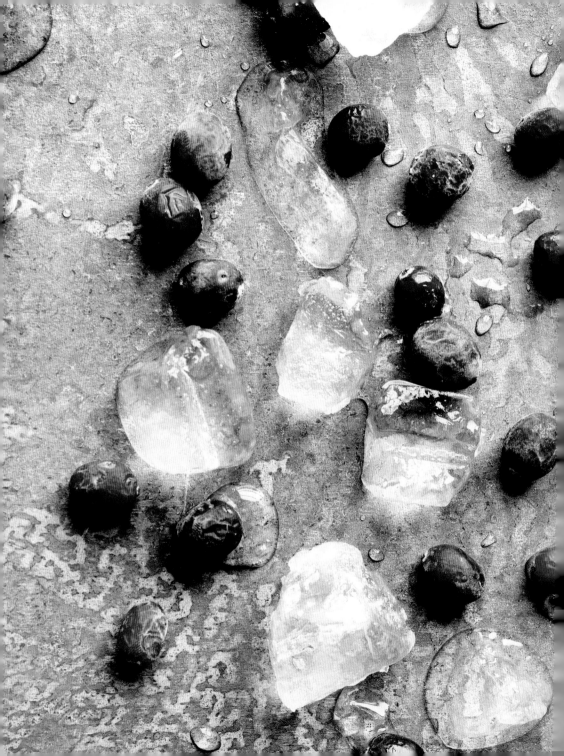

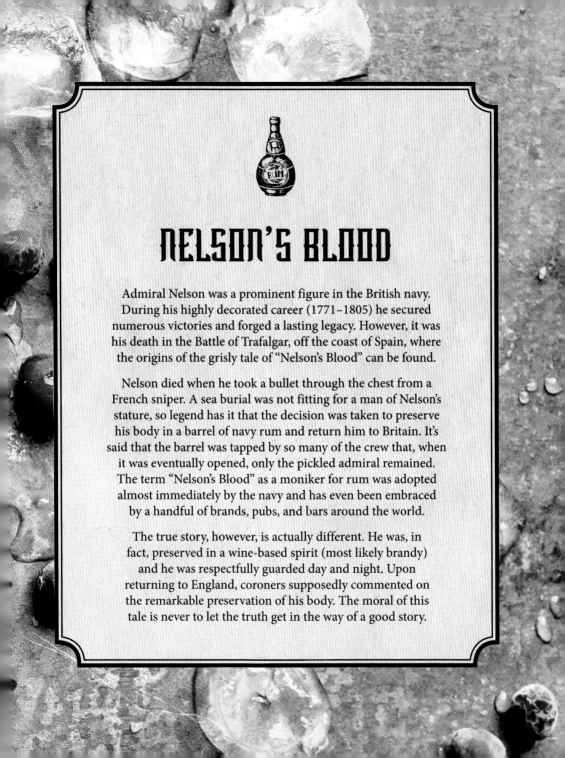

NELSON'S BLOOD

Admiral Nelson was a prominent figure in the British navy. During his highly decorated career (1771–1805) he secured numerous victories and forged a lasting legacy. However, it was his death in the Battle of Trafalgar, off the coast of Spain, where the origins of the grisly tale of "Nelson's Blood" can be found.

Nelson died when he took a bullet through the chest from a French sniper. A sea burial was not fitting for a man of Nelson's stature, so legend has it that the decision was taken to preserve his body in a barrel of navy rum and return him to Britain. It's said that the barrel was tapped by so many of the crew that, when it was eventually opened, only the pickled admiral remained. The term "Nelson's Blood" as a moniker for rum was adopted almost immediately by the navy and has even been embraced by a handful of brands, pubs, and bars around the world.

The true story, however, is actually different. He was, in fact, preserved in a wine-based spirit (most likely brandy) and he was respectfully guarded day and night. Upon returning to England, coroners supposedly commented on the remarkable preservation of his body. The moral of this tale is never to let the truth get in the way of a good story.

PARISIAN BLONDE

Serves 1

—

Ingredients

¾ ounce dark rum

¾ ounce orange curaçao

¾ ounce cream

orange slice, to garnish

1. Shake the dark rum, orange curaçao,
and cream over cracked ice until well frosted.

2. Strain into a chilled cocktail glass
filled with ice. Garnish with an orange slice.

ANKLE BREAKER

Serves 1

—

Ingredients

1¾ ounces dark rum

¾ ounce cherry brandy

¾ ounce lime juice

1 teaspoon simple syrup

1. Shake the rum, cherry brandy, lime juice,
and simple syrup over cracked ice until well frosted.

2. Strain into a chilled cocktail glass.

LOUNGE LIZARD

Serves 1

Ingredients

1¾ ounces dark rum

¾ ounce amaretto

cola

1. Shake the rum and amaretto over cracked ice until well frosted. Strain into a chilled cocktail glass.

2. Top off with cola and stir gently.

CIDER BREEZE

Serves 1

Ingredients

¾ ounce coconut rum

sparkling cider

apple slice, to garnish

1. Add the rum to a chilled cocktail glass that is filled halfway with ice cubes.

2. Top off with the cider. Garnish with an apple slice.

PALM BEACH

Serves 1

—

Ingredients

1½ ounces white rum

1½ ounces gin

1½ ounces pineapple juice

pineapple, to garnish

1. Shake the rum, gin, and pineapple juice
over cracked ice until well frosted.

2. Strain into a chilled cocktail glass
filled with ice. Garnish with pineapple.

PLANTER'S COCKTAIL

Serves 1

—

Ingredients

1½ ounces rum

juice of ½ lime

1½ ounces pineapple juice

1 teaspoon simple syrup

1 teaspoon grenadine

1 dash Angostura bitters

fruit slices, to garnish

1. Shake the rum, pineapple juice, lime juice, simple syrup, grenadine, and Angostura bitters together.

2. Pour into a chilled cocktail glass and garnish with fruit slices.

OCEAN BREEZE

Serves 1

—

Ingredients

¾ ounce white rum

¾ ounce amaretto

½ ounce blue curaçao

½ ounce pineapple juice

club soda

1. Shake the white rum, amaretto, blue curaçao, and pineapple juice over cracked ice until well frosted. Strain into a chilled cocktail glass.

2. Top off with club soda.

RUM 'N' CURRANT

Serves 1

—

Ingredients

¾ ounce dark rum

½ ounce black currant cordial

lemonade

1. Shake the rum and black currant cordial over cracked ice until well frosted. Strain into a chilled cocktail glass.

2. Top off with lemonade.

SPACE ODYSSEY

Serves 1

Ingredients

¾ ounce golden rum

2 dashes Angostura bitters

cocktail cherries

ginger beer

1. Mix the rum and bitters in a chilled cocktail glass filled with cracked ice and cocktail cherries.

2. Top off with ginger beer.

TAMARA'S TIPPLE

Serves 1

—

Ingredients

1¾ ounces dark rum

¾ ounce crème de cacao

cola

lemon slices

1. Shake the rum and crème de cacao over
cracked ice until well frosted. Strain into
a chilled cocktail glass filled with ice.

2. Top off with cola and garnish with slices of lemon.

THE DEVIL

Serves 1

—

Ingredients

¾ ounce dark rum

½ ounce red vermouth

black olive, to garnish

1. Shake the rum and vermouth over cracked ice until well frosted. Strain into a chilled cocktail glass filled with ice.

2. Garnish with a black olive.

Chapter 3

INGENIOUS MIXES

With the increased popularity of rum cocktails, mixologists across the globe have been challenged to create the next big thing: to take classic ingredients and fuse them with unexpected flavors—and the results are as exciting as they are delicious. Here you'll find the Beer & Rum Flip, Salted Caramel Rum Hot Cocoa, Winter Daiquiri, and Mermaid Water. Surprising, intriguing, and out of the ordinary, these cocktails won't disappoint.

RUM COBBLER

Serves 1

Ingredients

3½ ounces whiskey barrel wood chips

1½ cups dark rum

splash grenadine

½ ounce maraschino liqueur

cocktail cherry, orange slices, and lime slices, to garnish

1. This cocktail takes 2 weeks to infuse and you will need a blowtorch. Lay the whiskey barrel chips on a metal tray and place on a heatproof surface.

2. Using a chef's torch, scorch all over the wood chips until about half have blackened. Put the scorched wood chips into a sterilized, sealable jar, then pour in the rum. Keep the rum bottle for later use. Mix and seal the jar. Leave in a cool place for 2 weeks.

3. After 2 weeks, strain the rum through a fine-mesh strainer. Fill an old-fashioned glass with ice. Pour in 1¾ ounces of the rum. The rest can be stored for up to 2 months.

4. Add the grenadine and maraschino liqueur and stir. Garnish with the cherry, orange, and lime.

WINTER DAIQUIRI

Serves 1

Ingredients

1¾ ounces golden rum

2 teaspoons runny honey

2 strips orange zest

1-inch piece cinnamon
stick, halved

1 thin slice fresh ginger

1 allspice berry, crushed

2 teaspoons fresh orange juice

2 teaspoons fresh lime juice

1 teaspoon water

1 teaspoon superfine sugar

large pinch ground cinnamon

1. Add the rum, honey, orange strips, cinnamon, ginger, and allspice to a small saucepan and warm gently together for 1–2 minutes. Remove from the heat and leave to cool for at least 1 hour, or longer if you have time, so that the flavors can infuse together.

2. When ready to serve, strain the infused rum into a cocktail shaker, reserving the aromatics. Add the orange and lime juices and cracked ice, then shake together gently until well frosted.

3. To "frost" the glass, add the water to a saucer. Add the sugar and ground cinnamon to a second saucer. Dip the rim of a cocktail glass first in the water, then in the sugar. Cut some of the reserved orange into thin strips and add to the glass with a long, thin sliver of the reserved cinnamon. Strain the daiquiri into the glass.

BLACKBERRY & MINT MOJITO

Serves 1

Ingredients

1 tablespoon fresh lime juice

1¾ ounces white rum

1¾ ounces blackberry mint syrup (see below)

fresh mint sprig

club soda, to taste

BLACKBERRY MINT SYRUP

10 large fresh mint leaves

¾ cup blackberries

¼ cup superfine sugar

1. To make the blackberry mint syrup, rub the mint leaves in your hands to release their flavor then add to the base of a small saucepan. Sprinkle in the blackberries then add the sugar and two ounces of water. Heat gently, stirring occasionally until the sugar has dissolved, then boil for 1 minute. Take off the heat and leave to cool for 30 minutes.

2. Press the blackberry mixture through a fine sieve to remove the blackberry seeds. Pour into a sterilized, sealable jar and chill in the refrigerator.

3. To make the cocktail, add the lime juice, rum, and blackberry mint syrup to a cocktail shaker with a handful of cracked ice. The rest of the blackberry mint syrup can be stored in the refrigerator for up to 3 days. Shake vigorously until well frosted. Pour into a chilled cocktail glass filled with ice and a sprig of mint. Top off with chilled club soda to taste.

CRANBERRY MULES

Serves 1

Ingredients

2 tablespoons cranberry
syrup (see below)

1¾ ounces white rum

3½ ounces ginger beer

frozen cranberries, to garnish

CRANBERRY SYRUP

1 cup frozen cranberries

½ cup superfine sugar

1 cup water

1. First make the cranberry syrup by adding the cranberries, sugar, and water to a small saucepan. Cook over low heat, stirring occasionally, until the sugar has completely dissolved, then increase the heat slightly and simmer for about 5 minutes or until the cranberries have burst and the liquid is thick and syrupy. Cover and leave to cool.

2. Puree if desired, then pour into a sterilized, sealable jar and chill in the refrigerator.

3. To make the cocktail, add 2 tablespoons of the cranberry syrup to a glass filled with ice. The rest of the syrup can be stored in the refrigerator for up to 3 days.

4. Add the white rum and ginger beer to a cocktail shaker with some cracked ice. Shake together until well frosted and frothy. Pour into the glass to create a two-tone effect. Finish with a few frozen cranberries.

THE DAILY RATION

No drink has stronger ties with the navy than rum.
The first official rum rations for British sailors
began in 1655 and continued up until 1970.

Fresh water never traveled well on ships and beer would often
sour, becoming a putrid barrel of rancid, stagnant filth, especially
when traveling in warmer parts of the world. Rum however,
thanks to its high alcoholic strength, would travel indefinitely.
Aside from its preserving qualities, it served another important
role—keeping up morale and offering much-needed respite from
what would have been for many a hard and uncertain life at sea.

The quantities of the rum ration varied over the centuries, because
fairly legitimate concerns were raised over the competency of
intoxicated crews, keeping in mind the ration was likely consumed
on top of more private stashes of rum. Admiral Edward Vernon
was responsible for a major change in the ration when he insisted
that the half-pint ration of rum be watered down and flavored with
lime in order to ward off drunkenness. The quantity of rum didn't
change, so the new drink was not badly received by the crew. Plus
the lime helped ward off scurvy, potentially helping to save lives.

The drink soon became known as "grog," taking its name from
Vernon's nickname "Old Grogman"—a name that he acquired
through routinely wearing a weatherproof jacket known then
as a "Grogman". Admiral Vernon, or "Old Grogman," could
arguably be credited for creating one of the first rum cocktails.

MANDARIN & LIME GINGER BEER

Serves 1

Ingredients

1 lime

½ mandarin orange

1¾ ounces dark rum

5 ounces ginger beer

lime wedges, to garnish

1. Cut the lime and mandarin orange into wedges.

2. Place the lime and mandarin orange into a cocktail shaker. Use a muddler for about 10 seconds to crush the fruit and to release its oils.

3. Add the rum and stir with a barspoon.

4. Pour the rum mixture into a Collins or highball glass.

5. Add a few ice cubes and top off with the ginger beer.

6. Garnish with lime wedges.

POLAR BEAR

Serves 1

—

Ingredients

1¾ ounces light rum

1¾ ounces advocaat

juice of 1 passion fruit, strained, seeds reserved to garnish

lemonade

1. Blend the rum, advocaat, and most of the passion fruit juice with crushed ice in a blender for about 10 seconds, until thick, and frothy.

2. Strain into a chilled cocktail glass filled with ice and top off with lemonade to taste.

3. Finally, swirl the remaining passion fruit juice with the reserved seeds on top of the ice.

CHAMBORD SOUR

Serves 1

—

Ingredients

¾ ounce Chambord
raspberry liqueur

¾ ounce rum

¾ ounce lemon juice

egg white

1 tablespoon simple syrup

blackberry, to garnish

1. Chill a coupe glass.

2. Put a handful of ice cubes into a cocktail shaker.
Pour the liquid ingredients over the ice cubes.

3. Shake the cocktail shaker vigorously until the mixture
creates foam. Strain into a chilled coupe glass.

4. Garnish the cocktail with the blackberry.

MERMAID WATER

Serves 1

Ingredients

1¾ ounces spiced rum

¾ ounce coconut rum

1 tablespoon fresh lime juice

6 ounces pineapple juice

fresh lime and lemon slices

2 teaspoons blue curaçao

small pineapple pieces,
peel left on, to garnish

1. Add the spiced rum, coconut rum, and lime juice to a cocktail shaker, then pour in the pineapple juice and add a handful of ice cubes. Shake vigorously together until well frosted.

2. Pour the rum mixture and ice into a tall glass and add lime and lemon slices. Drizzle the blue caraçao over the top.

3. Thread the pineapple pieces onto a toothpick and arrange on the top of the glass.

BEER & RUM FLIP

Serves 4

—

Ingredients

1½ cups stout

1¾ ounces dark rum

1¾ ounces maple syrup

2 eggs

1 teaspoon nutmeg,
to garnish

1. Gently heat the stout in a medium saucepan over a medium heat.

2. Pour the rum and maple syrup into a blender. Crack in the eggs.

3. When the stout has almost come to a boil, pour it carefully into the blender and blend for 30 seconds, or until the contents are nice and frothy.

4. Divide the flip between four snifter glasses and garnish each drink with a little nutmeg.

GOLD COFFEE

Serves 1

—

Ingredients

¾ ounce dark rum

¾ ounce orange curaçao

2½ ounces strong, cold
black coffee

1 scoop vanilla ice cream

2 teaspoons strained
passion fruit juice

1. Put the dark rum, curaçao, and coffee
into a blender. Add some ice cubes
and blend until slushy.

2. Pour into a chilled glass, add the ice cream,
and spoon over the passion fruit sauce.

HONEY, PEACH & AGAVE INFUSION

Serves 1

Ingredients

1 lime

2 ripe peaches, cut into wedges

10 peppercorns

2 star anise

½ vanilla bean, split

1 cinnamon stick

2 tablespoons agave syrup

2 tablespoons honey

1½ cups tequila

¾ ounce rum

¾ ounce lime juice

1 egg white

¾ ounce triple sec

peach slice, to garnish

1. This cocktail takes 1 month to develop. Place the peach wedges in a sterilized, sealable jar. Add the peppercorns, star anise, vanilla, cinnamon, agave, honey, and tequila. Keep the tequila bottle for later use.

2. Mix and seal. Leave in a cool place for a month. After a month, strain the tequila through a fine-mesh strainer. Once strained, pour the tequila back into its bottle. Place ¾ ounce of the tequila into an ice cube-filled cocktail shaker. The rest of the tequila can be stored for up to 2 months. Add the rum, lime juice, egg white, and triple sec.

3. Shake vigorously until well frosted. Strain into an ice-filled old-fashioned glass and garnish with the peach slice.

NIRVANA

Serves 1

—

Ingredients

1¾ ounces dark rum

½ ounce grenadine

½ ounce tamarind syrup

1 teaspoon simple syrup

grapefruit juice

1. Shake the rum, grenadine, tamarind syrup, and simple syrup over ice until well frosted.

2. Strain into a chilled cocktail glass filled with ice.

3. Top off with grapefruit juice.

POLYNESIAN SOUR

Serves 1

—

Ingredients

1¾ ounces light rum

½ ounce guava juice

½ ounce lemon juice

½ ounce orange juice

1. Put a handful of crushed ice, light rum,
guava juice, lemon juice, and orange juice
into a blender and blend until smooth.

2. Strain into a chilled cocktail glass filled with ice cubes.

SALTED CARAMEL RUM HOT COCOA

Serves 4

Ingredients

2 tablespoons granulated sugar

1 tablespoon water

salt flakes

7 ounces milk

1½ ounces semisweet chocolate, broken into pieces

1 teaspoon unsweetened cocoa powder

pinch ground cinnamon

¾ ounce dark rum

shaved or grated semisweet chocolate, to garnish

mini marshmallows, to serve (optional)

1. Add the sugar and water to a small heavy saucepan and heat gently, without stirring, until the sugar has completely dissolved.

2. Bring to a boil and boil rapidly for 4–5 minutes, without stirring, until the simple syrup begins to turn golden around the edges. Keep a very close eye on it at this stage and continue to heat until the syrup is a rich golden brown all over.

3. Remove the pan from the heat, add the salt, swirl to mix, then gradually pour in the milk. Stand well back as you add the milk as the syrup can splatter. Put the pan back over low heat and stir to mix the caramel and milk together. Add the chocolate. Stir the cocoa powder with a little water to make a paste and add it with the cinnamon. Keep stirring until smooth.

4. When the chocolate mix is hot but not boiling, stir in the rum, warm together, then pour into four heatproof glass mugs. Sprinkle with shaved or grated chocolate. Add mini marshmallows, if desired.

ZOMBIE

Serves 1

Ingredients

1¾ ounces dark rum

1¾ ounces white rum

¾ ounce golden rum

¾ ounce triple sec

¾ ounce lime juice

¾ ounce orange juice

¾ ounce pineapple juice

¾ ounce guava juice

1 tablespoon grenadine

1 tablespoon orgeat syrup

1 teaspoon Pernod

fresh mint sprig and
pineapple wedge,
to garnish

1. Shake the liquid ingredients over crushed ice until well frosted.

2. Strain into a chilled cocktail glass.

3. Garnish with the fresh mint and the pineapple wedge.

Chapter 4

MYSTERIOUS BLENDS

The mystery of a good thriller is often alluded to in the name—a dash of imminent danger, an air of the supernatural, or a good dose of suspense. The recipes in this chapter certainly conjure up this sense of intrigue and peril in their ambiguous names and dramatic appearance. Here, you'll find the Black Tower, White Lion, Green Devil, and Dragon Lady—proceed with caution...

FLAMING MAI TAI

Serves 1

Ingredients

¾ ounce dark rum

½ ounce triple sec

½ ounce brandy

4 ounces pineapple juice

½ ounce orgeat

⅓ cup chopped fresh pineapple

½ teaspoon cinnamon

½ ounce 151 overproof rum

mint leaves, to garnish

1. Shake the rum, triple sec, brandy, pineapple juice, and orgeat over ice until well frosted.

2. Strain the cocktail into a heatproof hurricane glass filled with ice cubes.

3. Place the chopped pineapple, cinnamon, and 151 rum into a mixing glass. Stir with a barspoon to combine.

4. Tilt the mixing glass and light the rum mixture with a long match. With care and using flame-resistant gloves, pour the lit rum mixture into the cocktail in the hurricane glass.

5. Allow the flames to die down and the drink to cool completely before drinking. Garnish with mint leaves.

BLACK TOWER

Serves 1

Ingredients

⅔ ounce dark rum

⅓ ounce whiskey liqueur

juice ½ lime

1 dash curaçao

club soda

lime slices, to garnish

1. Shake the rum, whiskey liqueur, lime juice, and curaçao well together over cracked ice and strain into a chilled tumbler filled with ice.

2. Top off with club soda and garnish with lime slices.

MYSTERIOUS

Serves 1

Ingredients

¾ ounce dark rum

¾ ounce orange curaçao

½ ounce coffee liqueur

½ ounce fresh orange juice

1 tablespoon heavy cream, to garnish

1. Shake dark rum, orange curaçao, coffee liqueur, and orange juice over ice until well frosted.

2. Strain into a chilled cocktail glass and top with cream.

RUM AND PIRACY

Ask someone to draw a pirate and you will almost certainly get all the classic features: the eye patch, peg leg, parrot on the shoulder, and, of course, a bottle of rum. The pirate stereotype has evolved over the decades, shaped through modern cinema and popular culture. But at least one part of the stereotype is pretty accurate—the rum.

In reality, pirates existed in a culture far removed from the stylized Hollywood interpretations. As social outcasts and people living on the edge, they would be happy drinking anything they could get their hands on. It just so happened that the majority of ships moving around the trade triangle between the Americas, Europe, and Africa would have been carrying rum, a universal currency of the time, so it was easy pickings.

However, some experts would argue that pirates were actually more fond of brandy. This isn't that surprising as, for large chapters of history, pirates were licensed to attack Spanish ships to help the British navy. These ships heading from Spain to the colonies probably would have been carrying high-quality grape-based alcohol. Whatever pirates were drinking, it's unquestionable that booze was at the heart of many pirate ships.

GREEN DEVIL

Serves 1

Ingredients

lime juice

confectioners' sugar

¾ ounce light rum

½ ounce blue curaçao

¾ ounce orange juice

lime slice, to garnish

1. Dip the rim of a large cocktail glass into lime juice and then into sugar to create sugar frosting.

2. Set aside to dry. Shake the light rum, blue curaçao, and orange juice over ice until well frosted.

3. Pour into the frosted glass and garnish with a slice of lime.

EYE-OPENER

Serves 1

Ingredients

¾ ounce rum

2 dashes crème de noyaux

2 dashes absinthe

2 dashes curaçao

1 egg yolk

1 teaspoon confectioners' sugar

1. Shake the rum, crème de noyaux, absinthe, curaçao, egg yolk, and confectioners' sugar over ice until well frosted.

2. Strain into a chilled cocktail glass.

TONGUE TWISTER

Serves 1

Ingredients

¾ ounce light rum

½ ounce coconut
cream liqueur

½ ounce orange curaçao

¾ ounce lemon juice

grated nutmeg, to garnish

1. Shake the light rum, coconut cream liqueur, orange curaçao, and lemon juice over cracked ice until well frosted.

2. Strain into a chilled cocktail glass filled with ice and sprinkle with grated nutmeg.

WHITE LION

Serves 1

Ingredients

1 dash Angostura bitters

1 dash grenadine

1¾ ounces white rum

¾ ounce lemon juice

1 teaspoon simple syrup

1. Shake the Angostura bitters, grenadine, white rum, lemon juice, and simple syrup over cracked ice until well frosted.

2. Strain into a chilled cocktail glass.

TIGER'S MILK

Serves 1

Ingredients

1¾ ounces golden rum

1¼ ounces brandy

1 teaspoon simple syrup

4 ounces milk

ground cinnamon and a
cinnamon stick, to garnish

1. Put the rum, brandy,
simple syrup, and milk into a
blender with crushed ice and
blend until well combined.

2. Pour into a chilled cocktail
glass. Sprinkle with ground
cinnamon and garnish
with a cinnamon stick.

ZOMBIE PRINCE

Serves 1

Ingredients

1 dash Angostura bitters

¾ ounce white rum

¾ ounce golden rum

¾ ounce dark rum

½ ounce lemon juice

½ ounce orange juice

½ ounce grapefruit juice

1 teaspoon packed brown sugar

1. Shake the Angostura bitters, white rum, golden rum, dark rum, lemon juice, orange juice, and grapefruit juice over cracked ice until well frosted. Then add the sugar.

2. Stir to mix well, then strain into a tall chilled cocktail glass filled with ice.

RAIL-ROADSTER

Serves 1

—

Ingredients

1 teaspoon fine zest of lime

1 teaspoon
confectioners' sugar

1¼ ounces white rum

½ ounce Galliano

¾ ounce lime juice

dry ginger ale

1. Mix the lime zest and sugar together.

2. Rub the rim of a glass with a little rum, then dip it
into the sugar to coat thoroughly. Set aside to dry.

3. Shake the white rum, Galliano, and lime juice
over cracked ice until well frosted.

4. Pour into the cocktail glass filled with ice
and top off with a little ginger ale.

FIREMAN'S SOUR

Serves 1

—

Ingredients

1¾ ounces white rum

1¼ ounces lime juice

1 tablespoon grenadine

1 teaspoon simple syrup

cocktail cherry, to garnish

1. Shake the white rum, lime juice, grenadine,
and simple syrup over cracked ice until well frosted.

2. Strain into a chilled cocktail glass and garnish with a cocktail cherry.

BIG CITY MIST

Serves 1

—

Ingredients

¾ ounce Irish Mist

¾ ounce dark rum

1¾ ounces passion
fruit juice

¾ ounce pink
grapefruit juice

1 dash grenadine

1. Shake Irish Mist, dark rum, passion fruit juice,
pink grapefruit juice, and grenadine over
cracked ice until well frosted.

2. Pour into a chilled cocktail glass filled with ice.

DRAGON LADY

Serves 1

Ingredients

¾ ounce golden rum

¾ ounce orange juice

1 dash curaçao

1 dash grenadine

Bitter Lemon, chilled

orange slice, to garnish

1. Stir golden run, orange juice, curaçao, and grenadine over cracked ice until well frosted.

2. Strain into a highball glass filled with ice and top off with bitter lemon.

3. Garnish with a slice of orange.

XYZ

Serves 1

—

Ingredients

½ ounce fresh lemon juice

½ ounce white rum

½ ounce Cointreau

lime slice, to garnish

1. Shake the lemon juice, white rum,
and Cointreau over ice until well frosted.

2. Strain into a chilled cocktail glass filled with ice and garnish with a slice of lime.

BEAUTIFUL DREAMER

Serves 1

—

Ingredients

1¾ ounces white rum

¾ ounce coconut cream,
beaten until creamy

¾ ounce guava juice

¾ ounce pineapple juice

melon or guava
slices, to garnish

1. Shake white rum, coconut cream, guava juice,
and pineapple juice over cracked ice until well frosted.

2. Pour into a cocktail glass filled with ice and garnish with fruit slices.

Chapter 5

ISLAND PARADISE

Transport yourself to total island paradise with the recipes in this chapter. Think sunshine, palm trees, and waves of turquoise water washing onto golden sand as you prepare fresh fruit and sunny mixers. Here, you'll find recipes like Tropical Sangria, Blue Hawaiian, Barbados Sunset, and Strawberry Colada that all conjure up idyllic vacation vibes with just a simple twist of the cocktail shaker.

PEACH DAIQUIRI

Serves 1

Ingredients

1¾ ounces white rum

¾ ounce lime juice

½ teaspoon simple syrup

½ peach, peeled,
pitted, and chopped

1. Put the white rum, lime juice, simple syrup, and peach in a blender and blend until smooth.

2. Pour, without straining, into a chilled cocktail glass filled with ice cubes.

STRAWBERRY COLADA

Serves 1

Ingredients

2½ ounces golden rum

3½ ounces pineapple juice

¾ ounce coconut cream

6 strawberries

pineapple wedge and
halved strawberry,
to garnish

1. Put the rum, pineapple juice, coconut cream, and cracked ice into a blender.

2. Add the strawberries to the blender. Blend until smooth.

3. Pour, without straining, into a chilled cocktail glass. Garnish with a pineapple wedge and strawberry half.

TROPICAL FRUIT PUNCH

Serves 6

Ingredients

1 small ripe mango

2 ounces lime juice

1 teaspoon finely grated fresh ginger

1 tablespoon packed light brown sugar

5 cups orange juice

5 cups pineapple juice

3 ounces white rum

fruit slices, to garnish

1. Put the mango, lime juice, ginger, and sugar into a blender and blend until smooth.

2. Add the orange juice, pineapple juice, and the rum and blend again for a few seconds until smooth.

3. Divide the crushed ice between six chilled cocktail glasses and pour the punch over it. Garnish with fruit slices.

TROPICAL SANGRIA

Serves 1

Ingredients

½ cup diced watermelon

⅓ cup diced pineapple

¼ small papaya, seeded, peeled, and diced

½ lime, cut into wedges

1¾ ounces golden rum

4 ounces Spanish white Rioja wine

3 ounces pineapple juice

2½–4 ounces chilled club soda or sparkling mineral water, to serve

1. Add the diced watermelon, pineapple, and papaya to a mason jar. Squeeze the juice from the lime over the top and add the squeezed wedges to the jar.

2. Pour over the rum, white wine, and pineapple juice and stir together. Screw on the lid, then chill in the refrigerator for 30 minutes, or longer if you have time, so that the flavors can infuse together.

3. When ready to serve, pour the club soda into the jar, stir together, then add ice cubes.

BAJAN SUN

Serves 1

—

Ingredients

¾ ounce white rum

¾ ounce mandarin brandy

¾ ounce orange juice

¾ ounce pineapple juice

splash grenadine

fresh pineapple slice and
cocktail cherry, to garnish

1. Shake the rum, brandy, orange juice, and
pineapple juice over cracked ice until well frosted.

2. Add the grenadine and shake vigorously.

3. Strain into a chilled cocktail glass and garnish with
a pineapple slice and cocktail cherry.

BLUE HAWAIIAN

Serves 1

—

Ingredients

1¾ ounces white rum

½ ounce blue curaçao

¾ ounce pineapple juice

½ ounce coconut cream

pineapple wedge, to garnish

1. Shake the rum, blue curaçao, pineapple juice, and coconut cream over cracked ice until well frosted. Strain into a chilled cocktail glass.

2. Garnish with the pineapple wedge.

BANANA COLADA

Serves 1

Ingredients

1¾ ounces white rum

3½ ounces pineapple juice

¾ ounce Malibu

1 banana, peeled and sliced

pineapple wedges, to garnish

1. Put the white rum, pineapple juice, Malibu,
sliced banana, and ice in a blender and blend until smooth.

2. Pour, without straining, into a chilled cocktail glass.
Garnish with pineapple wedges.

CUBAN SPECIAL

Serves 1

—

Ingredients

1¾ ounces white rum

¾ ounce lime juice

1 tablespoon pineapple juice

1 teaspoon triple sec

pineapple wedges, to garnish

COCO ROCO

Serves 1

Ingredients

1¾ ounces fresh coconut juice

½ ounce white rum

½ ounce apricot brandy

½ ounce coconut milk

1. Put the fresh coconut juice, white rum, apricot brandy, coconut milk, and cracked ice into a blender and blend until smooth.

2. Pour into a chilled cocktail glass filled with ice.

RUM AND REVOLUTION

The trade in molasses to make rum was widespread, and distilleries making rum were cropping up all over New England.

Ships loaded with molasses were making their way from the French West Indies to the rum distillers of New England, and the profits were tidy. A gallon of French molasses was typically sold for 1 shilling—but once fermented and distilled into rum, it was selling for 6 shillings a gallon. Numerous New England distilleries and French colonies were profiting at the expense of the British Crown. The French molasses was leaving such a bad taste in the mouths of the British government that it made efforts to stop the illicit ships heading north. Naval efforts had failed, so the British responded with hefty taxes on the New Englanders—taxes which encouraged smuggling and corruption amongst the colonial officials. This encouraged the idea of independence.

One champion of American independence, a young George Washington, was running for election in the Virginia House of Burgesses in 1755. Records suggest he served up 28 gallons of straight rum, along with 50 gallons of rum punch and plenty of wine and beer to locals during his campaign. His crowd-pleasing efforts led to a landslide victory. After independence and his presidency was achieved, George went on to set up his own distillery.

CALYPSO STING

Serves 1

Ingredients

¾ ounce dark rum

¾ ounce Malibu

½ ounce orange curaçao

½ ounce orange juice

1 dash fresh lime juice

tonic water

1 dash Angostura bitters

cherry and a slice of
lime, to garnish

1. Shake the dark rum, Malibu, orange curaçao, orange juice, and lime juice over cracked ice until well frosted. Strain into a chilled cocktail glass filled with ice and top off with tonic water.

2. Finish with a drop or two of Angostura bitters, and garnish with a cherry and a lime slice.

BARBADOS SUNSET

Serves 1

Ingredients

1¼ ounces golden rum

¾ ounce coconut rum

1¾ ounces orange juice

1¾ ounces pineapple juice

1 dash strawberry syrup

fruit slices, to garnish

1. Shake the golden rum, coconut rum, orange juice, pineapple juice, and strawberry syrup over cracked ice until well frosted. Strain into a chilled cocktail glass.

2. Add more ice and garnish with slices of fruit.

AMIGOS PIÑA COLADA

Serves 4

Ingredients

4 ounces white rum

8 ounces pineapple juice

5 ounces coconut cream

1¾ ounces dark rum

4¼ ounces light cream

pineapple wedges, to garnish

1. Put the white rum, pineapple juice, coconut cream, dark rum, cream, and ice into a blender and blend until smooth.

2. Pour, without straining, into chilled cocktail glasses and garnish with pineapple wedges.

BANANA DAIQUIRI

Serves 1

Ingredients

1¾ ounces white rum, chilled

½ ounce triple sec, chilled

½ ounce lime juice

½ ounce light cream, chilled

1 teaspoon simple syrup

banana, peeled and sliced

lime slice, to garnish

1. Put white rum, triple sec, lime juice, light cream, and simple syrup into a blender and blend.

2. Add the banana and blend until smooth.

3. Pour, without straining, into a chilled cocktail glass.

4. Garnish with a lime slice.

POLYNESIA

Serves 1

—

Ingredients

1¾ ounces white rum

1¾ ounces passion
fruit juice

¾ ounce lime juice

1 egg white

1 dash Angostura bitters

1. Shake the rum, passion fruit juice, lime juice,
and egg white over cracked ice with a dash of
Angostura bitters until well frosted.

2. Strain into a chilled cocktail glass.

PINEAPPLE PLANTER'S PUNCH

Serves 1

—

Ingredients

¾ ounce white rum

¾ ounce pineapple juice

juice of ½ lime

½ ounce curaçao

1 dash maraschino liqueur

kiwi and pineapple
slices, to garnish

1. Shake the white rum, pineapple juice, lime juice, curaçao, and maraschino liqueur over cracked ice until well frosted. Strain into a chilled cocktail glass.

2. Garnish with the fruit slices.

SAILOR'S RUM PUNCH

Serves 1

Ingredients

¾ ounce lemon juice

1¾ ounces simple syrup

2½ ounces strong rum

few shakes of Angostura bitters

3½ ounces fruit juice

fruit pieces, to garnish

1. Shake the lemon juice, simple syrup, rum, and Angostura bitters over cracked ice until well frosted. Set aside to let the flavors develop.

2. To serve, stir in the fruit juice and pour into a chilled cocktail glass with a little more ice. Garnish with fruit pieces.

Chapter 6

CREATIVE COOLERS

Warmer weather calls for an ice-cold cooler, and the recipes in this chapter provide a creative selection of perfectly chilled drinks. Think easy-breezy combined with a touch of ingenuity here. Frozen cocktails, such as the Frozen Daiquiri and Palm Breeze, provide instant icy satisfaction, while Piña Colada Pops and Mojito Pops combine classic cocktails with the novelty of a strictly adults-only ice pop.

MANGO FREEZE

Serves 4

Ingredients

6 ounces golden rum

3½ ounces mango juice

3½ ounces fresh orange juice

¾ ounce simple syrup

good squeeze lemon juice

1 egg white

lemonade

mango slices, to garnish

1. Put the golden rum, mango juice, orange juice, simple syrup, lemon juice, and egg white in a blender and blend with ice until frothy and frozen.

2. Pour into frozen cocktail glasses and top off with lemonade. Garnish with a slice of mango.

FROZEN DAIQUIRI

Serves 1

Ingredients

1¾ ounces white rum

¾ ounce lime juice

1 teaspoon simple syrup

lime slice, to garnish

1. Put the rum, lime juice, and simple syrup in a blender with ice and blend until slushy and frozen.

2. Pour into a chilled cocktail glass and garnish with a lime slice.

JAMAICAN COOLER

Serves 1

Ingredients

1¼ ounces Jamaican rum

club soda

lemon slices, to garnish

1. Pour the rum into a chilled cocktail glass filled with ice cubes.

2. Top off with club soda and garnish with lemon slices.

MOJITO POPS

Makes 8

Ingredients

juice of 6 limes

2½ cups chilled club soda

1¼ cups fresh mint leaves

3 limes, cut into wedges

½ cup superfine sugar

4 tablespoons white rum

YOU WILL ALSO NEED

8 (½-cup) ice pop molds

8 ice pop sticks

1. Put the lime juice and club soda into a measuring cup and stir together well.

2. Stir in the mint leaves, lime wedges, sugar, and rum. Using a "muddler," or thick wooden spoon or mallet, mash together all the ingredients until well blended.

3. Pour the mixture into 8 (½-cup) ice pop molds. Divide the lime wedges and mint leaves evenly between them. Insert the ice pop sticks and freeze for 10–12 hours, or until firm.

4. To unmold the ice pops, dip the frozen molds into warm water for a few seconds and gently release the pops while holding the sticks.

STRAWBERRIES & CREAM

Serves 1

—

Ingredients

¾ ounce light rum, chilled

¾ ounce grapefruit
juice, chilled

¾ ounce heavy cream

5–6 large strawberries,
hulled (save one to serve)

1. Put the light rum, grapefruit juice, cream, and strawberries
in a blender with cracked ice and blend until slushy and frozen.

2. Pour into a chilled cocktail glass and garnish
with the remaining strawberry.

FROZEN STRAWBERRY DAIQUIRI

Serves 1

———

Ingredients

1¾ ounces white rum

¾ ounce lime juice

1 teaspoon simple syrup

7 large strawberries, hulled
(save one to serve)

1. Put the white rum, lime juice, simple syrup,
and strawberries in a blender with ice and blend until slushy.

2. Pour into a chilled cocktail glass and garnish
with the reserved strawberry.

JOSIAH'S BAY FLOAT

Serves 1

Ingredients

1¾ ounces golden rum

¾ ounce Galliano

1¾ ounces pineapple juice

¾ ounce lime juice

4 teaspoons simple syrup

champagne

pineapple shell, to serve

fruit slices, to garnish

1. Shake the golden rum, Galliano, pineapple juice, lime juice, and simple syrup over cracked ice until well frosted.

2. Strain into the pineapple shell.

3. Top off with champagne and garnish with fruit slices.

THE FUTURE OF RUM

The trend for cocktails using carefully selected ingredients and unique flavor combinations has pushed traditional rum drinks to exciting new creations. With a growing demand for quality liquor and cocktails with provenance, new producers and craft distillers are constantly concocting inventive and high-quality rums.

The sugar industry in the West Indies and the old colonies has been declining for decades, but as a result, established rum producers are responding by securing their own plantations and sugarcane needs, adding more provenance and control over their processes in turn. With controlled and well-cultivated cane fields comes better cane juice and better rums, which is great news for consumers.

With time, the industry is hopeful that more solid and official guidelines surrounding the production of Caribbean rum will emerge. Clear guidelines surrounding the sweetening of rums prior to bottling and aging in turn allows for greater transparency in the industry, ultimately helping consumers to make informed choices.

So long as the world keeps producing sugar, sugarcane-based liquor will always be with us. Innovative brands will keep pushing boundaries for new audiences, and armed with clear definitions and a focus on quality, they will appeal to the serious liquor enthusiasts of the world.

RUM SWIZZLE

Serves 1

—

Ingredients

1¾ ounces dark rum

¾ ounce fresh lime juice

½ ounce simple syrup

2–3 dashes Angostura bitters

1. Put the dark rum, lime juice, simple syrup,
and Angostura bitters in a blender with ice
and blend until frothy and part frozen.

2. Pour into an iced tumbler with more ice to taste.

FROZEN PINEAPPLE DAIQUIRI

Serves 1

—

Ingredients

1¾ ounces white rum

¾ ounce lime juice

½ teaspoon pineapple syrup

⅓ cup finely chopped
fresh pineapple

pineapple wedges, to garnish

1. Put the white rum, lime juice, pineapple syrup, and chopped pineapple in a blender with ice and blend until slushy.

2. Pour into a chilled cocktail glass. Garnish with pineapple wedges.

CARIBBEAN BLUES

Serves 1

Ingredients

¾ ounce white rum

½ ounce blue curaçao

good squeeze lime juice

¼ ounce simple syrup

club soda

3 frozen lime slices,
to garnish

1. Mix the white rum, blue curaçao, lime juice, and simple syrup in chilled cocktail glass with a few ice cubes.

2. Top off with club soda and garnish with frozen slices of lime.

PLANTER'S PUNCH REFRESHER

Serves 1

Ingredients

1¾ ounces rum

1¾ ounces lime juice

1–2 teaspoons grenadine

1 dash Angostura bitters

club soda

1. Shake the rum, lime juice, grenadine, and Angostura bitters over cracked ice until well frosted.

2. Strain into a chilled cocktail glass filled with ice.

3. Top off with club soda.

BEACH BUM

Serves 1

—

Ingredients

¾ ounce dark rum

¾ ounce peach brandy

¾ ounce lime juice

½ mango, pitted,
peeled, and chopped

mint, to garnish

1. Put the dark rum, brandy, lime juice, and mango into
a blender and blend at a slow speed for about 10 seconds.

2. Pour into a chilled cocktail glass filled with ice
and garnish with a sprig of mint.

FROZEN PEACH DAIQUIRI

Serves 1

Ingredients

½ peach, pitted and chopped

1 ¾ ounces white rum

¾ ounce lime juice

1 teaspoon simple syrup

peach slice, to garnish

1. Put the peach, white rum, lime juice, and simple syrup into a blender with cracked ice and blend until slushy.

2. Pour into a chilled cocktail glass. Garnish with a peach slice.

PIÑA COLADA POPS

Makes 8

Ingredients

3½ cups finely diced pineapple

7 ounces coconut milk

6 tablespoons superfine sugar

2 ounces Malibu

YOU WILL ALSO NEED

8 (½-cup) ice pop molds

8 ice pop sticks

1. Drop a tablespoon of the diced pineapple flesh into each of the 8 (½-cup) ice pop molds.

2. Put the remaining pineapple flesh in a blender with the coconut milk, sugar, and Malibu and blend until smooth.

3. Strain using a fine metal strainer, pressing down to extract all the juice. Discard the solids. Pour the mixture into the ice pop molds. Insert the ice pop sticks and freeze for 6–8 hours, or until firm.

4. To unmold the ice pops, dip the frozen molds into warm water for a few seconds and gently release the pops while holding the sticks.

CASABLANCA

Serves 1

Ingredients

2½ ounces white rum

3½ ounces pineapple juice

1¾ ounces coconut cream

pineapple wedge, to garnish

1. Shake white rum, pineapple juice, and coconut cream over cracked ice until well frosted.

2. Strain into chilled cocktail glasses with ice.

3. Garnish with pineapple.

PALM BREEZE

Serves 1

Ingredients

¾ ounce white rum

¾ ounce gin

1¾–2½ ounces pineapple juice

fresh pineapple slice, to garnish

1. Shake the white rum, gin, and pineapple juice over cracked ice until well frosted.

2. Strain into chilled cocktail glasses.

3. Garnish with a slice of fresh pineapple.

INDEX

—

This edition published by Cottage Door Press, LLC, in 2022.
First published 2017 by Parragon Books, Ltd.

Copyright © 2022 Cottage Door Press, LLC
5005 Newport Drive, Rolling Meadows, Illinois 60008

Introduction by Joe Clark
Recipes by Sara Lewis
Photography by Mike Cooper. Additional photos used under license from Shutterstock.com.
Cover design by Bert Fanslow. Cover art used under license from Shutterstock.com.

ISBN 978-1-64638-498-3

Printed in China

Love Food™ is an imprint of Cottage Door Press, LLC.
Parragon® and the Parragon® logo are registered trademarks of Cottage Door Press, LLC.

Notes for the Reader

This book uses standard kitchen measuring spoons and cups. All spoon and cup measurements are level unless otherwise indicated. Unless otherwise stated, milk is assumed to be whole, eggs are large, individual vegetables are medium, and pepper is freshly ground black pepper. Unless otherwise stated, all root vegetables should be peeled prior to using. People with nut allergies should be aware that some of the prepared ingredients used in the recipes in this book may contain nuts.

Garnishes, decorations, and serving suggestions are all optional and not necessarily included in the recipe ingredients or method. The times given are only an approximate guide. Preparation times differ according to the techniques used by different people and the cooking times may also vary from those given. Optional ingredients, variations, or serving suggestions have not been included in the time calculations.

Please consume alcohol responsibly.